Invisible ME
THE BEAUTY OF BEING HIDDEN IN GOD

I0234071

KESHIA STAPLE

Unless otherwise indicated, **all** Scripture quotations are taken from the *Holy Bible*, New Living Translation, copyright © 1996, 2004, 2015 by Tyndale House Foundation. Used by permission of Tyndale House Publishers, Inc., Carol Stream, Illinois 60188. All rights reserved.

Scripture quotations marked AMP are taken from **the** Amplified Bible Copyright © 2015 by The Lockman Foundation, La Habra, CA 90631. All rights reserved.

Copyright © 2018 by Keshia Staple

Book Cover created by: Gracious Grafx – www.graciousgrafx.com

Driadonna Roland - Editor

Interior Design and Editing: Barracks Publishing International
iambevtheeditor@gmail.com

All Rights Reserved. This book or any portion thereof may not be reproduced or used in any form or any manner whatsoever without the express written permission of the author except for the use of brief quotations in a book review. Please direct all inquiries to: stapled2gether@gmail.com.

ISBN-13: 978-0-692-17822-5

Printed in the United States of America

Dedication

This book is dedicated to the One who saw me when no one else did – Thank you Jesus!

And to my son, Kamal. Greater works shall you do. Love you always!

~Mommy

Acknowledgements

To my husband, Mr. Staple, affectionately called Kevan; I love you more than words can describe. I could not have done this without you. You're the definition of what it means to be *supportive*. Thank you for believing in me, praying for me, and loving me so deeply.

To my mother in the Gospel, Joan Grey. I can write an entire book about the love and support you've shown me throughout the years. Your fasting, your prayers, your consistency, your dependency, your strength, and your encouraging words will not be wasted. Thank you for always being that reminder… that God can.

To my mentor, Nia S. Kelly (sigh). This journey would not have been possible without you. You helped me to break through barriers, limitations and held me accountable to the process. You Rock!!!

To my Auntie Sharon, you have always been a strong woman role model in my life. Your beauty and go getter mentality has always set standards for me to follow. You may not say much, but your life speaks volumes.

ACKNOWLEDGEMENTS

To my midwives in this season, Nikkie "Take ACTION" Pryce and Beverly "Girl You Better PUSH" Barracks—lol. You both pushed me further than I thought I could go. Thank you for believing in me ESPECIALLY on days when I didn't believe in myself. I am Forever Grateful.

Last but not least, to my family (whether blood related, close-friends, in-laws or family in Christ), I appreciate each one of you that have taken the time to pour into me. Whether you prayed, made me laugh, inspired, encouraged, etc... THANK YOU!

Foreword

Remember the name *Keshia Staple*, as she debuts into the Literary Arena with an impactful power punch of a book, *Invisible Me*. This book will show you that our experiences are truly designed to be a catalyst in the lives of others because we are all destined to win regardless of how we begin this game of life. It will show you that each trial, tribulation or challenge that we face in life will end as a testimony for someone else when you walk with God. I believe that by the end of Invisible Me, Keshia's transparency will open the door to true Freedom.

I applaud *Keshia* for sharing her testimony while being unapologetic, transparent, upfront, honest, but no longer *Invisible*. *Invisible* Me can be used to set the captives free when unexpected sudden storms of life manifest; unfortunately, your situation doesn't make you unique. I hope her heartfelt testimony will motivate each reader to reach beyond their limitations.

Invisible Me will allow you to reflect-back to those moments and situations when you felt *Invisible*; the moments where you may have felt isolated, unwanted, unloved, *but longed to be* accepted and relevant. *Invisible*

FOREWORD

Me will challenge you to be who God preordained you to be.

*T*hroughout *these Chapters, Keshia's* testimony touched me deeply, as I am sure it will you as well; we ALL have more in common than we do differences. Allow the words on the pages of *Invisible* Me to minister to you, as they did to me, and will to so many. If you don't already, this book will help you to seek a personal relationship with God through Jesus Christ our Savior and heal you from being *Invisible; a* very insightful read.

Beverly E. Barracks, Author of
I AM the Name with Power (31 Days Devotional)

Endorsement

Invisible Me... At some point in our lives we have all felt alone, forgotten, *invisible,* and one of the first lies the enemy tells us, in the midst of these times, is that your struggle is unique to you alone, and no one would understand even if you could find the courage to speak about it; *Invisible Me,* dispels that myth within the first few pages.

Keshia Staple does not judge, condemn or insult, instead she inspires with humility and a quiet strength, and an honesty that is bold, refreshing and instantly relatable. *Keshia* recounts the intimate details of her pain and struggles instead of carrying them in shameful silence; in a sincere and selfless effort to help the reader get past their own hurdles. Her willingness to speak about her past hurts and current difficulties helps you to realize you're not alone, your pain is not in vain and does not have to define you and most importantly she reminds us so affectionately; God has not Forgotten You.

Karla Halsall,
Freelance Editor/Proofreader

Table of Contents

Dedication ii
Acknowledgements iv
Foreword vi
Endorsement viii
Introduction 1
Chapter One "Hidden for a Purpose" 15
Chapter Two "Beauty in the Eyes of the Beholder" 23
Chapter Three "He Knows My Name" 31
Chapter Four "Rejected for a Cause" 35
Chapter Five "Hide & Seek" 45
Chapter Six "Hidden Treasure in Earthen Vessels" 51
Chapter Seven "Come Out Come Out Wherever You Are" 55
Letter from Keshia 69
Scriptures to Remember 71
About the Author 77

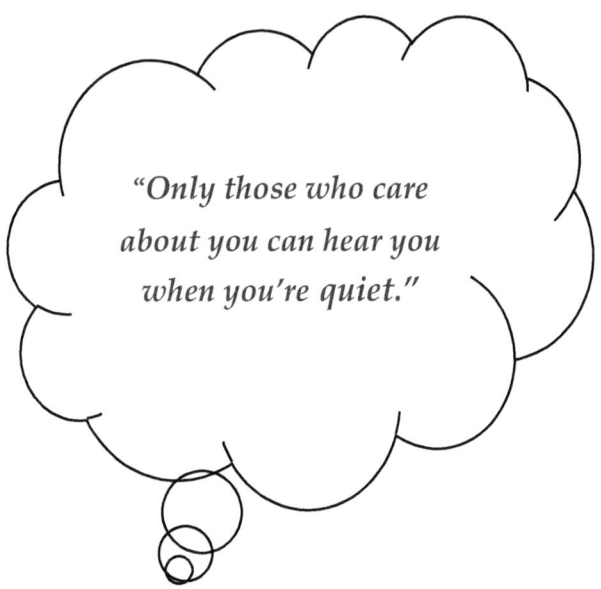

"Only those who care about you can hear you when you're quiet."

Introduction

Invisible: adj. *unable to be seen; not visible to the eye.*

Does the word *invisible* mean anything to you? Is it a word you often toss around in your mind to help describe the feelings you are battling? Are you familiar with feeling unseen, overlooked, invaluable, alone, rejected, despised? If you answered yes to any of these, then know, you're reading the right book at the right time. Not only are you reading the right book, but you are not alone, and help is here. For years, I've been where you are, battling the agonizing daily routine of feeling *invisible*, but by the Grace of God through Faith, I overcame this battle when I discovered whose I am and that my source and my worth is in the Great I AM that I AM.

Does that mean the attacks don't still happen? Thoughts of inferiority and mediocrity? Of course not, they happen all the time simply because we have an enemy that is resilient and refuses to give up. *1 Peter 5:8* says, *"Stay alert! Watch out for your great enemy, the*

INTRODUCTION

devil. He prowls around like a roaring lion, looking for someone to devour." But the wonderful thing about this ongoing battle is that we also have an Advocate—the *Holy Spirit* which brings us into truth and knowledge of how to defeat our enemies. This book's main objective is to help you conquer these silent issues before they conquer you.

My Story

Growing up, I never thought I would live past my early 20's. I thought I would die of a broken heart or take my own life. Although I experienced many gruesome things that no child should ever go through such as, molestation, neglect, verbal and physical abuse, things didn't take a turn for the worse until I was 19 years old. While visiting my parents' home for a spring break vacation, I was kidnapped and driven to a dark alley where I was raped by a man I barely knew. It was a few weeks before my 20th birthday and I didn't imagine that my transition from being a teenager would have been so depressing. At the time of the incident, my entire family was inside of our Miami home. I stepped outside for only a moment, to retrieve something from a person who portrayed himself to be friendly. I even left my front door slightly ajar because I intended to go right back in.

INTRODUCTION

But when I walked outside, I was tricked into reaching into the backseat of his vehicle to retrieve what I came out to get. As I reached in, he pulled off and headed towards the first dark alley he could find.

After the violation took place, he dropped me back off in the front of my house; I remember feeling like a zombie. I couldn't find an emotion to attach to the act; I just felt empty and as dry as the desert. As I walked towards my front door, I realized that it was still ajar. I was in total shock to find that as I walked through the front door, everyone in the house was still in their place of comfort and no one noticed I was missing for more than an hour, suffering the most horrific violation.

I was stiff-cold in that moment, but began to feel some sort of emotions, and those emotions did not stem from the rape. My sadness stemmed from feeling *invisible* my entire life and now on the brink of transitioning into my 20's, still battling with this rejection. I had already spent my existence thus far, feeling as if I was walking alone without anyone to love and protect me. Something so severe had happened that I should have been able to run to my family for support and protection, but that wasn't available to me.

I marked myself from that moment on as damaged goods. A woman with no worth, no purpose, simply here

INTRODUCTION

on earth by mistake. An orphan without a care and a hope. Can I let you in on a secret? When I was raped, I felt like God hated me. I couldn't understand why He would allow this to happen. I didn't grow up in a Christian household, but I believed in God. I just thought He didn't believe in me. I was so broken and just wanted to feel safe, to feel valued, to be seen by those closest to me. The light was missing from my eyes and as the days passed, I broke completely down.

Hope had left my body, and I just couldn't believe that no one would take the time out to see that I was going under. I didn't even report the rape because I felt like I deserved anything bad that happened to me. Quickly, depression and suicidal thoughts flooded my mind and I couldn't handle it. I allowed my hurt feelings and the mentality that *"nobody loves me"* take me to places no one should ever go to. Self-pity was in the driver's seat and things really got out of control.

The Encounter That Changed My Life

I managed to make it through another two years of life while battling depression and a few suicide attempts by the Grace of God. My depression spiraled down into a dark hole and I no longer had a will to leave my home which eventually led to me dropping out of college. I

INTRODUCTION

would sleep all day and party all night to suppress the pain that I was feeling on the inside. I had no family around to support me and had two friends that I hung out with who had no idea that I was struggling with depression. I acted like I had it all together on the outside because I was too ashamed to admit my brokenness to anyone. Not to mention, the enemy convinced me that no one would even care.

When I was 22 years old, I met a sweet, handsome, charming, loving and kind young man while vacationing in Jamaica. This man has now been my husband of eight years. When Kevan and I first met, it was like a breath of fresh air. I had never met anyone who showed such great concern and care for my well-being that it almost seemed too good to be true. I didn't think a relationship between us would work because in my mind, I was too toxic. By that time in my life, I was so tired of pretending that I had it all together so much so that being a negative and dark person was the norm. I was also intimidated by his family; they were Christians and tightly knitted together with love. They had lots of family gatherings with loads of laughter, singing, dancing and praying. All the things I wasn't accustomed to—growing up.

As time passed in our relationship, I began to feel like a different person. I was constantly surrounded by

INTRODUCTION

people who carried the love of God and gave it so freely. The darkness in me didn't stand a chance. This goes to show that you must be very careful of the company you keep and entertain. *1 Corinthians 15:33* says, *"Don't be fooled by those who say such things, for 'bad company corrupts good character.'"*

I grew up in a very toxic environment and eventually I became just that. I have four brothers yet, I always felt like an only child. My father hardly came around to visit and no matter how many times I called, left voice messages or pleaded for visits, I eventually accepted the reality that I would never be daddy's little girl. Already coupled with verbal and physical abuse at an early age, before adding molestation to the equation, you can understand my awkwardness of suddenly being connected to a family that expressed so much love.

In 2009, Kevan decided to completely give his life over to the Lord. I didn't understand the plan of salvation at the time, but I was happy that he wanted to serve the Lord. I thought for sure that he was going to break things off with me and find a nice young lady in the church who was more suited for his new lifestyle and standards. After all, I was the party girl with tons of emotional problems that needed to be worked through.

INTRODUCTION

I remember late one night, receiving a phone call from him and I immediately thought to myself, something must be wrong as he didn't sound like his usual self. He told me he called just to pray with me and encourage me. I was totally in shock as I had-never had a guy that I was dating "pray for me." Though it was strange and very uncomfortable for me, I allowed it and received the prayer.

The next night, he called and did the same thing; he prayed and encouraged me to come to Christ. I didn't know how to respond to this. After all, I didn't understand God's forgiveness, mercy and grace and I just thought that the hurt, the pain and rejection that I've experienced in life was because God was mad at me. I saw no beauty in what I had been through. Just lots of scars and open wounds that couldn't seem to heal.

The late-night calls to pray and to encourage me continued for a couple of weeks. I would cry secretly while on the phone because I couldn't understand this love this very sweet man, my future husband, had for me. I couldn't understand why he cried when I cried or why he would even care about the pain that I was experiencing on the inside. I mean, he's a macho man who loves sports and works hard with his hands, but he had a soft spot for me. Eventually, I accepted an

INTRODUCTION

invitation to attend church with him and the rest is history. That Sunday, I unexpectedly gave my life over to Christ and was baptized in the Name of Jesus. Until this day, my husband still sits up late at night crying out to God on my behalf.

I might have felt insignificant and *invisible* my entire life, but God turned a nightmare into a beautiful story. My husband taught me the works of prayer and faith in God and I began to dig deep into the Word of God which helped uproot all the negativity that was within me. **John 1:5** says, *"The light shines in the darkness, and the darkness can never extinguish it."* So, the dark parts of me became exposed to the light of Christ and healing began; little-by-little and day-by-day, and I began to submit to God and watched Him work miracles in my life.

Suddenly, the things that use to hurt me no longer had power over me. Self-pity went out the door and I began to walk free. I also submitted to spiritual and wise counsel which helped me get to that place of freedom. I want to pause this story for a moment to explain something very important.

If you're hurting and need help, say something. Don't wallow in self-pity and allow the enemy to push you so deep into depression that suicide becomes your

INTRODUCTION

only option. It's reported that 25 million Americans suffer from depression each year. Over 50 percent of all the people who die by suicide suffered from major depression.[1] Stop worrying about the few people that can't see your value and focus on the One who Created you with great purpose. Be aggressive about your deliverance and seeking help. Also, accountability is key; find somebody that you can trust and talk to concerning your depression. Seek counseling and mix it with lots of prayer and the Word of God.

1 Corinthians 10:13 says, *"The temptations in your life are no different from what others experience. And God is faithful. He will not allow the temptation to be more than you can stand. When you are tempted, he will show you a way out so that you can endure."*

You are not alone, and God can and will deliver you.

Sometimes I can't believe that I survived such a dark time in my life, but I acknowledge that my being here today is just what we call Grace and Purpose from God. I trusted God to do something in me that I couldn't do for myself. I figured that if He allowed me to live even through those dark periods of my life, delivered me from depression, suicidal thoughts and attempts, that it was

---

[1] https://www.theovernight.org/index.cfm?useaction=cms.page&id=1034

INTRODUCTION

for a great purpose. Some things are unexplainable, but I knew God was the One bringing me out of darkness. My bad past was not a sign that God wasn't with me, instead it was the exact opposite.

Psalm 27:10— *"if my father and mother abandon me, the Lord will hold me close."*

Turning Around for Your Good

Today, I have a ministry, *Stapled 2gether*, that helps young hurting women put back the broken pieces of their lives using the Word of God, daily inspiration and mentorship. I no longer look at my past as a curse, but as a hidden blessing. You may be saying to yourself, *"this girl is insane thinking rape, molestation, rejection and abandonment issues are a hidden blessing,"* but hear me out for a second. If I didn't experience the mess that I went through, how could I really connect with other women who are suffering with the same issues? How could I be truthful and minister to people with compassion that are facing rejection from a loved one or peers? The answer is simple; I wouldn't be able to. My body may have been attacked, but God kept my mind in perfect peace for this very reason. What the enemy meant for evil, God surely turned it around for my good and His Glory and He can and will do the same for you.

INTRODUCTION

Throughout this book, I want to help you build confidence in the God that Created you. We all have a Purpose here on this earth and we are valuable to God even when the people around us don't acknowledge it. Sometimes, people's oversight of you may not be intentional on their part, but intentional on God's part for the building of character and even your protection. God wants to reveal the beauty in being hidden in Him, as God is no respecter of persons. Meaning, what God has done for me and so many others, He can most definitely do it for you. This book is designed to help you see that God is with you, He sees you, He acknowledges your pain and He wants to deliver you.

As you journey with me throughout this book, we will walk through biblical stories and personal testimonies to help you reflect and find purpose and beauty in your time of affliction. Though man may not recognize you or even call you by name, God sees and knows exactly who you are. He Created you in His Image, and my hope and prayer for you is that through this book, you will receive Power and Authority to rise above every painful and destructive thought that has held you captive in your life. God desires good things for all of us, so let the healing begin.

INTRODUCTION

So, take a deep breath, grab a pen and a notepad, a prayerful spirit, Oh, and don't forget to take a renewed mind into this process; you got this…

You are Special!

"Just because you're not visible to people doesn't mean you're not valuable to God."

Chapter One
"Hidden for a Purpose"

Imagine this: A beautiful dinner party is being hosted in your home. The finest of the finest china is being put out and the chef is making filet mignon with all your favorite side dishes. Not only is the town's elite invited to this party, but famous actors, music artists and the President of the United States of America is going to be there as well. How exciting! But there's one little catch—you're not invited.

1 Samuel 16:1-13
Samuel Anoints David as King

>"Now the Lord said to Samuel, "You have mourned long enough for Saul. I have rejected him as king of Israel, so fill your flask with olive oil and go to Bethlehem. Find a man named Jesse who lives there, for I have selected one of his sons to be my king."
>
>But Samuel asked, "How can I do that? If Saul hears about it, he will kill me."
>
>"Take a heifer with you," the Lord replied, "and say that you have come to make a sacrifice to the Lord. Invite

Jesse to the sacrifice, and I will show you which of his sons to anoint for me."

So Samuel did as the Lord instructed. When he arrived at Bethlehem, the elders of the town came trembling to meet him. "What's wrong?" they asked. "Do you come in peace?"

"Yes," Samuel replied. "I have come to sacrifice to the Lord. Purify yourselves and come with me to the sacrifice." Then Samuel performed the purification rite for Jesse and his sons and invited them to the sacrifice, too. When they arrived, Samuel took one look at Eliab and thought, "Surely this is the Lord's anointed!"

But the Lord said to Samuel, "Don't judge by his appearance or height, for I have rejected him. The Lord doesn't see things the way you see them. People judge by outward appearance, but the Lord looks at the heart."

Then Jesse told his son Abinadab to step forward and walk in front of Samuel. But Samuel said, "This is not the one the Lord has chosen." Next Jesse summoned Shimea,[a] but Samuel said, "Neither is this the one the Lord has chosen." In the same way all seven of Jesse's sons were presented to Samuel. But Samuel said to Jesse, "The Lord has not chosen any of these." Then Samuel asked, "Are these all the sons you have?"

"There is still the youngest," Jesse replied. "But he's out in the fields watching the sheep and goats."

"Send for him at once," Samuel said. "We will not sit down to eat until he arrives."

So Jesse sent for him. He was dark and handsome, with beautiful eyes.

And the Lord said, "This is the one; anoint him."

So as David stood there among his brothers, Samuel took the flask of olive oil he had brought and anointed David with the oil. And the Spirit of the Lord came powerfully upon David from that day on. Then Samuel returned to Ramah."

Although I can't say I know exactly how David felt not being invited to such an important gathering in his own house, I can definitely identify with being rejected and selected last. Often, people who struggle with feeling *invisible* are discounted in comparison to others who have *"the look."* Do you know what I mean? They walk a certain way, talk a certain way, dress a certain way, carry certain gifts and are automatically selected as *"the one."* I just love in **1 Samuel 16:7** when God speaks to Samuel and says, *"Don't judge by his appearance or height, for I have rejected him. The Lord doesn't see things the way you see them. People judge by outward appearance, but the Lord looks at the heart."*

David was discredited by his own family members simply because he was the youngest and worked in the field with animals. David might not have been as polished as his older brothers, but the Lord said to the Prophet Samuel, *"This is the one; anoint him."*

I can only imagine the look on David's father and brothers faces while the oil was being poured on him. Imagine their surprise to know that the one they looked at as a little Shepard boy was a King! Talk about hidden in plain sight. *Matthew 20:16* says, *"So those who are last now will be first then, and those who are first will be last."* David was called-out last by men, but he was chosen first as God's anointed.

Jesus says in *Matthew 21:42*, *"… Didn't you ever read this in the Scriptures? The stone that the builders rejected has now become the cornerstone. This is the LORD's doing, and it is wonderful to see."* David being called-out last should bring hope to you and me. God hid him in the fields where he got experience taking on lions and bears and caring for the sheep.

David may not have recognized then what God was preparing him for, but David had kingdom purpose long before he was even announced publicly. God chose to keep David hidden until that appointed time, much like God is keeping some of us hidden for a period. Don't get discouraged when people don't call you to the forefront or acknowledge you as "the one."

Let me ask you this, have you ever worked with a manager or supervisor that is clueless on how to operate in that position? I'll give you one better, have you been more qualified and skilled than your boss that signs your paycheck? Nothing is worse than having a title without the wisdom and knowledge to operate in that position. I believe God has some of you in a hidden place for a divine purpose and you're not happy about it. God is making sure you're equipped for that place, that position, that ministry that He's bringing you into.

David's rejection benefited him in the end. There was beauty in him being called-out last. David went on to be one of the most talked about Kings in the Bible; from slaying Goliath, winning many battles, to writing some of the most beautiful psalms and prayers in the Bible. David went down in history known as a man after God's own heart despite his rejection and own personal pitfalls. I believe that David's success all points back to his training days in the field. By now, you should be changing your outlook on your humble beginnings.

So, keep working in the fields and gaining the experience you will need for whatever it is that God has called you to. If you rush the process, you'll miss the

training and won't be equipped when God promotes you to the forefront. *Proverbs 18:16* says, *"Giving a gift can open doors; it gives access to important people."* Stay hidden until God calls you out of hiding. Being *invisible* is not so bad once you discover the purpose behind it, so remain hidden and stay focused; you won't regret it.

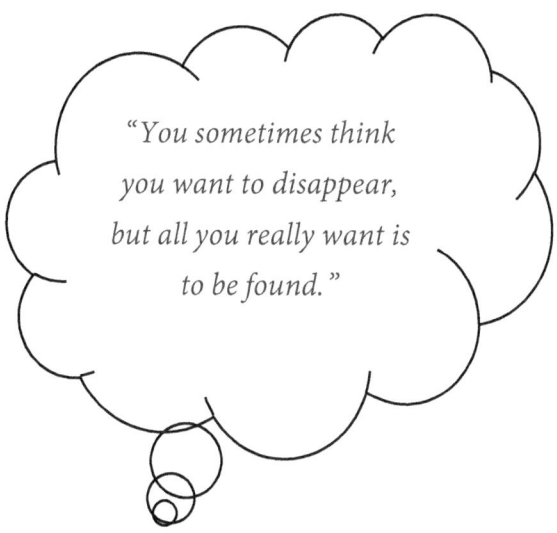

"You sometimes think you want to disappear, but all you really want is to be found."

Chapter Two
"Beauty in the Eyes of the Beholder"

Romans 5:8— *"But God showed his great love for us by sending Christ to die for us while we were still sinners."*

Coming to Christ was the best decision I could ever make, but it was still a journey to forgive others and myself for things of my past. My public worship and private moments with the Lord would often be interrupted by the tormenting thoughts of who I used to be and people's opinions of me. Initially, I didn't grab ahold of **2 Corinthians 5:17** which says, *"This means that anyone who belongs to Christ has become a new person. The old life is gone; a new life has begun!"*

I allowed people's views to barricade me into a box that I couldn't fight my way out of. They said, *"You're weak! You're not a leader. Your mind is all messed up. The potential is there, but I don't think you'll make it too far. You're not smart enough. You don't sound like a preacher. You're not anointed. You're not beautiful enough."* Sounds shocking, but it's true and the list of mean and discouraging words goes on and on. That was some people's view of me, but that didn't have to be my reality.

I often encounter young women that struggle with this same exact issue. Viewing themselves in the lens of negative people or crippling thoughts from the devil verses the lens of God who loves us even when we're wrapped, tangled and tied up in sin. One story in the Bible that I used to encourage myself and others is the woman with the *alabaster jar* in the book of **Luke Chapter 7.**

Luke 7:36-50—

Jesus Anointed by a Sinful Woman

"One of the Pharisees asked Jesus to have dinner with him, so Jesus went to his home and sat down to eat. When a certain immoral woman from that city heard he was eating there, she brought a beautiful alabaster jar filled with expensive perfume.

Then she knelt behind him at his feet, weeping. Her tears fell on his feet, and she wiped them off with her hair. Then she kept kissing his feet and putting perfume on them. When the Pharisee who had invited him saw this, he said to himself, "If this man were a prophet, he would know what kind of woman is touching him. She's a sinner!"

Then Jesus answered his thoughts. 'Simon,' he said to the Pharisee, 'I have something to say to you.'

"Go ahead, Teacher," Simon replied.

Then Jesus told him this story: 'A man loaned money to two people—500 pieces of silver to one and 50 pieces to the other. But neither of them could repay him, so he kindly forgave them both, canceling their debts. Who do you suppose loved him more after that?'

Simon answered, "I suppose the one for whom he canceled the larger debt."

"That's right," Jesus said. Then he turned to the woman and said to Simon, 'Look at this woman kneeling here. When I entered your home, you didn't offer me water to wash the dust from my feet, but she has washed them with her tears and wiped them with her hair. You didn't greet me with a kiss, but from the time I first came in, she has not stopped kissing my feet. You neglected the courtesy of olive oil to anoint my head, but she has anointed my feet with rare perfume.

"I tell you, her sins—and they are many—have been forgiven, so she has shown me much love. But a person

who is forgiven little shows only little love." Then Jesus said to the woman, "Your sins are forgiven."

The men at the table said among themselves, "Who is this man, that he goes around forgiving sins?"

And Jesus said to the woman, 'Your faith has saved you; go in peace.'"

One of my favorite quotes was written by Author, Margaret Wolfe Hungerford, *"beauty is in the eye of the beholder."* When I read the story of the woman with the *alabaster jar*, this quote often invades my thoughts. What I love most about God is that His thoughts towards us never changes and are so pure. We often think that living a life of perfection is what makes God love us, but on the contrary.

In **Isaiah 55:9** it says, *"For just as the heavens are higher than the earth, so my ways are higher than your ways and my thoughts higher than your thoughts."* Need I say more?

We don't have to earn God's love; it's given freely (no strings attached). King David says it best in **Psalms 139:8**— *"If I go up to heaven, you are there; if I go down to the grave, you are there."* Whether we choose God or deny Him, He still loves us. Real FREEDOM is when we

discover how much God Loves Us. That's my prayer, that we all come to the knowledge of how deep God's Love is for Us. Amen!

I often wondered why I would stoop to a level of viewing myself the way other people saw me or believe satan's lies. As I began to search myself, I quickly figured out I was nursing old wounds of rejection and was clinging to the words I should have released. They were tools sent by the devil to discourage and abuse me.

What old wounds are you holding onto that are crippling your thoughts about yourself?

Reading this story in **Luke 7** made me realize that no matter the sinful state we're in, Jesus still loves us and that we shouldn't allow any religious leaders, friends, family or especially the devil make us feel less than what God called us to be. I quickly learned that riding on the coattail of people's approval would have me high and lifted up one day and, on another day, low down hearing shouts of "crucify her." It's very pessimistic and damaging to see yourself the way everyone else may see you especially if people's vision of you is outside of the vision of God. What we call beautiful may be ugly to God. What we call blessings could be a curse. And what we see as disastrous is beautiful in God's sight because it's developing us.

The woman with the *alabaster jar* knew who she was and what she had done in her past, but she showed great strength and faith by pressing past the naysayers to get to Jesus. Jesus, the one who saw her as beautiful and said, "her sins—and they are many—have been forgiven," while "they" called her otherwise. Whose voice are you listening to today? I remember feeling so insignificant in life. There was not an area in my life that I didn't wrestle with. I struggled, I cried, and I just couldn't see myself as valuable to a single soul; not even to God.

This all began to manifest because I allowed negative seeds to be planted in me by people who couldn't find the beauty in anything; not even themselves. That is why the Word of God is so important when dealing with any form of rejection. Without the word hidden in your heart, you don't have a shot at winning the war. It's better to see yourself and measure yourself based on the mirror of the Word of God and not in the eyes of the negative beholder.

God, being truly loving and merciful, will always tell you the truth. And the truth for me wasn't that I wasn't beautiful inside and out; it wasn't even that I was insignificant or didn't belong, but that I was a precious jewel created by Him and for a great purpose. The truth has always been and forever will be that *I Am special. I*

Am anointed. I Am powerful. I Am strong and not weak. *I Am fearfully* and *wonderfully made. I Am valuable and I Am chosen.* These are some of the things you must begin to declare over your life again to walk in Victory. You have to check people's fruit and not be so quick to pick up labels that God hasn't given to you. Don't be afraid to challenge words spoken to you if they don't line up with the Word of God NO MATTER whom it's coming from. Speak life over yourself and counteract every negative word that makes you feel *invisible*.

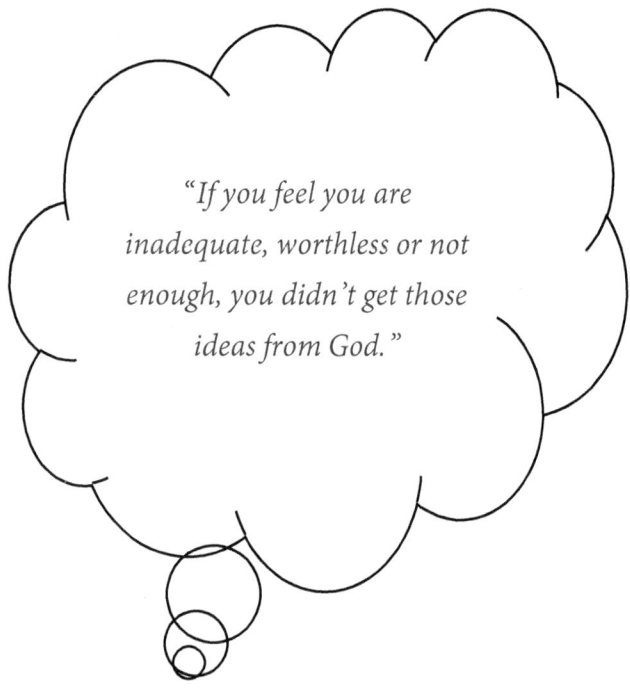

"If you feel you are inadequate, worthless or not enough, you didn't get those ideas from God."

Chapter Three
"He Knows My Name"

Moses, Moses. Jacob, Jacob. Samuel, Samuel. Abraham, Abraham. Simon, Simon. Saul, Saul. I think you get the picture — these are names of the people in the Bible who viewed themselves as insignificant in some shape or form, yet, God knew their names. He Called them at pivotal times in their lives when they felt *invisible* and unworthy of the Call. I want to ask you a question: How can you be insignificant when the BIGGEST celebrity in Heaven and Earth knows your name? I mean, He calls you by your government first and last name, and all your street nicknames (lol). How would you feel if you were walking in a crowd and *Denzel Washington* called you by name? Overjoyed; I would only guess. So, what about the Ruler of this Earth, the One who Created the Heavens and the Moon, the Stars and the Seas? In ***Isaiah 49:15-16,*** it says:

> "Never! Can a mother forget her nursing child?
> .... Can she feel no love for the child she has borne?

But even if that were possible,
.... I would not forget you!
See, I have written your name on the palms of my hands.
.... Always in my mind is a picture of Jerusalem's walls in ruins."

God has our names engraved in the palm of His hands. We are way too valuable to Him to just be forgotten. Now I know, some of you reading may say, 'If God finds us so special, then why do I feel so forgotten and alone?' I know the struggle all too well. Without an active mother or father in my life, I took it all as God abandoning me. That's why it is so important to dig deep into the Word of God *(you're going to hear me say this often – you can only find Truth about who you are in the Word of God)*. If you don't hide the word in your heart, when the enemy shows up and he will, you will not have any weapons to fight with.

The Truth is in the Word of God, not in your feelings. There were times when I felt like I didn't have a purpose, like God had abandoned me and didn't remember me; but that was totally opposite of God's thoughts toward me.

Luke 12:7 says, *"Even the very hairs of your head are all numbered."*

Matthew 28:20 says, "Lo, I am with you always, even unto the end of the world."

Psalm 27:10 says, *"Even if my father and mother abandon me, the LORD will hold me close."* And lastly,

Jeremiah 29:11 says, *"For I know the plans I have for you, says the LORD. They are plans for good and not for disaster, to give you a future and a hope."*

WOW! I'm so amazed as I go back over these scriptures. The promises that are held in them are so reassuring and inspiring. These words from the Lord apply to you (no man excluded) and will take you to new heights and depths if you only BELIEVE. Before we go any further, I just feel led to pray for you.

Let Us Pray…

Father, as we continue to dive into Your Word, I pray that the hearts of the people reading this will receive great breakthroughs in their minds and in their thinking. Lord, help us to know without a shadow of a doubt that Your Promises are sure and we can depend on Your Word. You have plans to prosper us and not to harm us, to give us an expected end. We thank You in advance for what You are doing and the transformation taking place even now. Thank You for hearing our cry, in Jesus' Name. Amen.

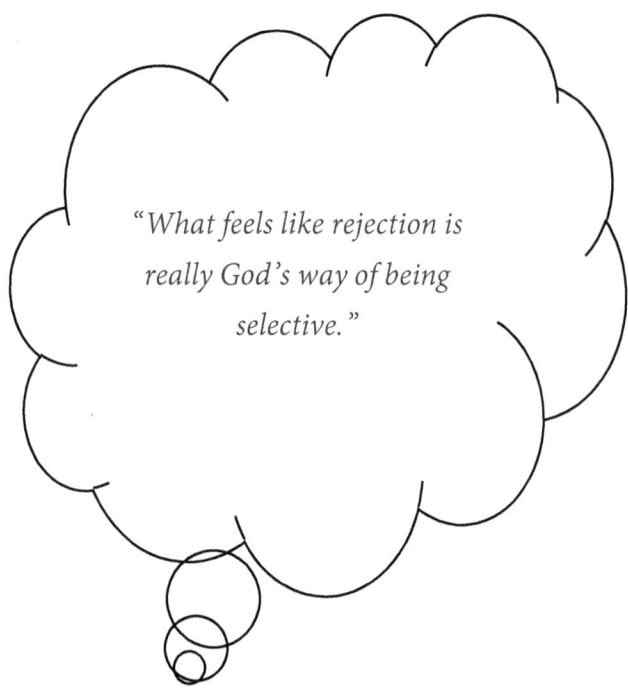

"What feels like rejection is really God's way of being selective."

Chapter Four
"Rejected for a Cause"

Genesis 37:3-4—*"Jacob[a] loved Joseph more than any of his other children because Joseph had been born to him in his old age. So one day Jacob had a special gift made for Joseph—a beautiful robe.[b] But his brothers hated Joseph because their father loved him more than the rest of them. They couldn't say a kind word to him."*

The story of Joseph is a perfect example of what rejected for a cause means. In **Genesis 37**, you get a glimpse of who Joseph was and the assignment that was upon his life. Joseph, being young, excited, full of energy and zeal for his future, would often share his dreams and visions with his brothers. But, there was a problem with that, Joseph's brothers were not very fond of him.

Genesis 37:4 says, *"But his brothers hated Joseph because their father loved him more than the rest of them. They couldn't say a kind word to him."*

REJECTED FOR A CAUSE

Ok, so let's pause right here... How many of you are making the same mistake of telling your dreams to people who secretly hate you and can't say a kind word about you behind your back? It's a hard question to take in with even harder answers to digest.

I often hear people pray against the spirit of rejection, but I'm convinced that rejection is a tool often used by God to build you and give you spiritual muscles more so than it is a "spirit" to bind and run out of your life. As a child, my father was not active in my life and my mother was a struggling single parent who focused on making sure her kids had clothes on their backs, food on the table and a roof over their heads. My mother wasn't the sentimental type, so I grew up a little on the rough side. I learned to hide my emotions and show no signs of weakness. I did my best to hold my head high, be tough and look out for my younger brothers. Although these were my outward characteristics, on the inside I was a broken young girl wanting her mommy and daddy.

I played tough for so long that I convinced myself that my parents' attention didn't matter to me. I felt *invisible* not just to the world but in my very inner circle. I was bruised on the inside and didn't know how to express it. I was often told over and over that I would never amount to anything in life (the devil is a liar!). I would often look up into the sky late at night and say, *"God, if you're real save me from this curse of being unseen."* I was hurt by the people around me and by this God that I heard so much about who supposedly loved good people. I often questioned, Why me? Why did I have to struggle with the feelings of rejection? Why did I have to go through the internal struggle of feeling *invisible*? What did I do wrong, God? What did I do wrong? I was emotionally tired, drained and began to give up on life.

The feelings of wanting to give up began to manifest on the outside. I just didn't care anymore. I wanted to die. I mean, nobody cared anyway, right? Not even God. As mentioned earlier, my feelings of rejection spiraled into feelings of depression and suicidal thoughts. I lost hope of ever being anything great or being seen for who I truly was. It was such a low and dark period in my life. I needed a turnaround and fast because I knew I was getting worse with no one around whom I could share my despair.

I remember breaking down one day and just feeling like I had no other option, but to talk to God even though I didn't know Him. I remember saying, *"God, if you can hear me, please, please turn things around for me. I don't want to be like everyone else."* I began to get confident with my talk with God and said, *"I WILL NOT be like everyone else; like those who treated me unfairly, but I will be different. I will make an impact on this earth."* I don't know where those powerful, earth-shaking, prophetic words came from, but now looking back, it is the proof and evidence that God was with me even then. I might not have understood then and you may not understand now, but God is always with us.

As the story of Joseph continues in the book of Genesis, Joseph's brothers sold him into slavery and told their Father that Joseph was dead. Joseph went from being sold into slavery, to being thrown into prison unwarrantedly, to being summoned before Pharaoh and put in charge of the whole land of Egypt. Joseph was made second-in-command of all of Egypt after going through years of suffering because of his loved ones. Talk about a real comeback story.

In *Genesis 41* where Joseph is now in prison for a crime he was not guilty of, the Bible says, that the Lord was with Joseph in prison and showed him His faithful love, and the Lord made Joseph find favor with the prison warden. Before long, the warden put Joseph in charge of all the other prisoners and over everything that happened in the prison. The warden had no more worries, because Joseph took care of everything. The Lord was with him and caused everything he did to prosper. Word got around to Pharaoh that Joseph had the gift of interpreting dreams and he wanted Joseph to interpret some dreams that he had that were troubling him.

Genesis 41:22-44— *"In my dream I also saw seven heads of grain, full and beautiful, growing on a single stalk. Then seven more heads of grain appeared, but these were blighted, shriveled, and withered by the east wind. And the shriveled heads swallowed the seven healthy heads. I told these dreams to the magicians, but no one could tell me what they mean."*

Joseph responded, "Both of Pharaoh's dreams mean the same thing. God is telling Pharaoh in advance what he is about to do. The seven healthy cows and the seven healthy heads of grain both represent seven years of prosperity. The seven thin, scrawny cows that came up later and the seven thin heads of grain, withered by the east wind, represent seven years of famine."

"This will happen just as I have described it, for God has revealed to Pharaoh in advance what he is about to do. The next seven years will be a period of great prosperity throughout the land of Egypt. But afterward there will be seven years of famine so great that all the

prosperity will be forgotten in Egypt. Famine will destroy the land. This famine will be so severe that even the memory of the good years will be erased. As for having two similar dreams, it means that these events have been decreed by God, and he will soon make them happen."

"Therefore, Pharaoh should find an intelligent and wise man and put him in charge of the entire land of Egypt. Then Pharaoh should appoint supervisors over the land and let them collect one-fifth of all the crops during the seven good years. Have them gather all the food produced in the good years that are just ahead and bring it to Pharaoh's storehouses. Store it away, and guard it so there will be food in the cities. That way there will be enough to eat when the seven years of famine come to the land of Egypt. Otherwise this famine will destroy the land."

"Joseph's suggestions were well received by Pharaoh and his officials. So Pharaoh asked his officials, 'Can we find anyone else like this man so obviously filled with the spirit of God?' Then Pharaoh said to Joseph, 'Since God has revealed the meaning of the dreams to you, clearly no one else is as intelligent or wise as you are. You will be in charge of my court, and all my people will take orders from you. Only I, sitting on my throne, will have a rank higher than yours.'"

Pharaoh said to Joseph, "I hereby put you in charge of the entire land of Egypt." Then Pharaoh removed his signet ring from his hand and placed it on Joseph's finger. He dressed him in fine linen clothing and hung a gold chain around his neck. Then he had Joseph ride in the chariot reserved for his second-in-command. And wherever Joseph went, the command was shouted, "Kneel down!" So Pharaoh put Joseph in charge of all Egypt. And Pharaoh said to him, "I am Pharaoh, but no one will lift a hand or foot in the entire land of Egypt without your approval."

Though Joseph may have felt betrayed, abandoned and alone while in captivity, it shows through his promotions that God's Favor was still with him everywhere he went; he was never forgotten, never ignored, nor neglected or unseen. Joseph's life should be an encouragement and hope for both you and I; this story never ceases to amaze me. *Selah.*

Like Job says, *"though He slay me, yet will I trust in Him."* Your story has been written by the greatest Author and your story will end well. If you are battling with rejection, rejoice! God is going to use that rejection as a stepping stone to elevate you. God is preserving you just like Joseph for something greater down the road.

Don't give up and don't lose hope. Joseph's rejection was for a greater cause and so is yours.

I didn't understand nor appreciate my rejection then, and it's understandable, but I sure do now. I get the opportunity every day to encourage and uplift people who are struggling with brokenness, and it's so fulfilling. The girl who once had no hope, no reason to live is now speaking life into so many. There's purpose for your pain and rejection. Stay the course no matter what.

Romans 8:28 declares, *"And we know that God causes everything to work together[a] for the good of those who love God and are called according to his purpose for them."*

God uses the very same tools that satan uses and turns them around for our good. He turns rejection into keys that help keep us away from people and situations that will deter or alter our destiny in a negative way. God uses rejection to ultimately put you in a place where He can shape and mold you without any harmful outside influence. God will place you on the backside of the wilderness like Moses to train and develop you for future service. So, don't be discouraged and don't throw in the towel. The God of Heaven sees your pain and your feelings of rejection and will make a way of escape; Trust the process and stay the course.

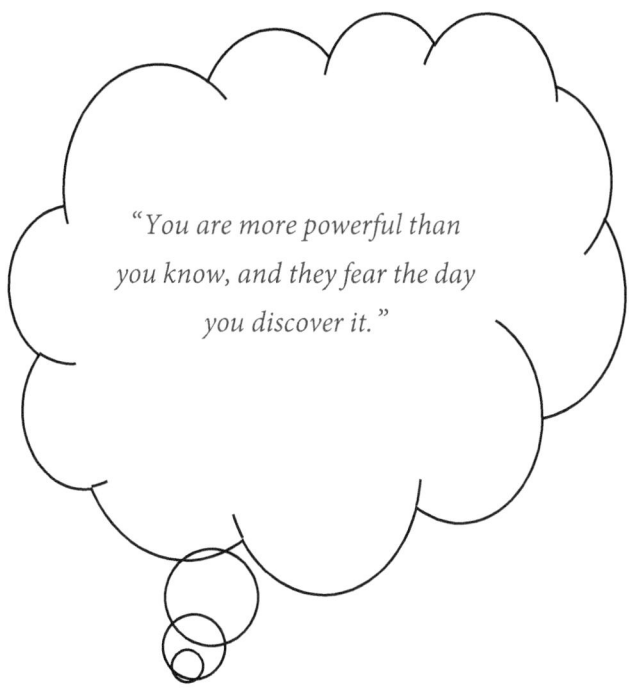

"You are more powerful than you know, and they fear the day you discover it."

Chapter Five
"Hide & Seek"

Matthew 7:7—*"Keep on asking, and you will receive what you ask for. Keep on seeking, and you will find. Keep on knocking, and the door will be opened to you.*

Now I know we live in a time and era when everything is about electronics and social media. But, I know there are a few people reading this book who can remember the good old days when we went outside to play. Tag, red light green light, hopscotch and the very large list goes on. But, who remembers playing hide and seek? Now, that was my game right there. I remember being good at it too. I would find the best hiding spots and my brothers could never find me…teehee; those were fun times. I always knew how to make myself *invisible* to the ones who wanted to find me.

Unfortunately, I sadly realized that even as an adult, I was still playing hide and seek whether I acknowledged it or not. Though time had passed and people and situations changed, I no longer was hiding from my little brothers, but I most certainly was playing hide and seek with God. I would say, *"Here I am Lord, ready for service. Use me, Lord. Send me, Lord,"* and when the time came to be used I would hide (if there is even such a thing as hiding from God). I hid because of insecurities I had deep down inside from how I viewed myself. I wholeheartedly wanted to be used, I longed for God to be proud of me, yet, the crippling words of others and how I viewed myself blocked my self-confidence, ministry and growth.

Finally, the day arrived when I became extremely frustrated and utterly fed up with myself and declared, "I will no longer continue to play these cat-and-mouse games with God." Because I would inevitably and secretly go and hide while I cried my eyes out; I felt empty from not living out my purpose. Taking responsibility for my destiny, I made the decision to go on a journey with the Lord and lock out every other influence around me.

My set time had arrived and I was so ready, focused and determined to hear directly from the throne room from heaven and get access to the encouragement I needed to hear in order to move. I started asking God to meet me in my private devotional time like He did with Adam in the Garden of Eden in the cool of the day.

Sometimes, we allow our sin to keep us running for cover from God when God wants us to run to Him.

I intentionally began taking my personal deliverance so seriously that I even hired a Christian life coach to help keep me accountable throughout my process. Can I tell you that every single time I sat before the Lord, He met me there and spoke reassuring words of life into me? I couldn't believe how the *Almighty God* would put me into His appointment book to encourage my soul.

We've been deceived into thinking that because we have problems and are not perfect people that God doesn't want to deal with us. Quite the opposite, in fact. Each time I sat with God and He spoke a word to me, it was confirmed not many days after. *Mind blowing!* It built my faith and confidence in such a way that I no longer hesitated walking in my calling because I was reassured by God.

Matthew 6:33 says, *"Seek the Kingdom of God above all else, and live righteously, and he will give you everything you need."*

Private moments like this kept me focused on my Kingdom agenda and helped me walk righteously.

In *Matthew 6:6* it says, *"But when you pray, go away by yourself, shut the door behind you, and pray to your Father in private. Then your Father, who sees everything, will reward you."* Hide and Seek is not just for young children playing outside in the yard, but for anyone who desires a close relationship with the Lord. I sense in my spirit that some of you may be saying *"I want a close walk with the Lord, but I don't know how."* Listen, the worst thing you can do is complicate something that has been made so simple.

Often times we use excuses such as *"I don't have the time or I don't know where to start."* Well, here's to no more excuses and here's an assignment to help get you started:

Be intentional about seeking private time with the Lord daily. Set a plan with dates and times that you will meet with the Lord in secret using the methods of Matthew Chapter 6.

Next, pray and ask the Lord to meet you there. Don't forget your worship and meditation music, pen, notebook and your Bible. Most importantly, go in with great expectation that the Lord will meet you there and speak to you. Be open and honest about how you feel and what you want out of your private time with Him. Go ahead, Hide and Seek Him out. You won't be disappointed.

"You're only invisible to those who don't deserve to see you."

Chapter Six
"Hidden Treasure in Earthen Vessels"

2 Corinthians 4:7(AMP)— *"But we have this* precious treasure [the good news about salvation] in [unworthy] earthen vessels [of human frailty], so that the grandeur and *surpassing greatness of the power will be [shown to be] from God [His sufficiency] and not from ourselves."*

I have a question for you. Yes, you. Don't look behind you (lol) I'm talking directly to you! My question is, do you know what you carry? Do you know what's on the inside of you?

God has planted some remarkable things on the inside of us that are like buried treasure. In this life we are on a hunt to discover where "X" marks the spot. Unfortunately, many people die without discovering their own unique treasure, but my hope and prayer throughout this book and chapter is that you will be inspired to pick up that treasure map also known as the Bible and launch out on your journey.

In *Jeremiah 33:3* it says—(AMP), *"Call to Me and I will answer you, and tell you [and even show you] great and mighty things, [things which have been confined and hidden], which you do not know and understand and cannot distinguish."*

This is just one of the great and amazing things about God. He is always willing and ready to engage in deep relationship with His Children. When we ask unanswered questions about our journey in life such as, *"Why are we here? What is my purpose? Why am I going through this?"* I think of this as looking for buried treasure without the map. It's often said that the richest place in the world is a graveyard because million-dollar and billion-dollar ideas, visions and dreams are all buried deep beneath the ground.

Another common mistake we make in treasure hunting is asking the wrong people for direction. We tend to ask or discuss road maps to life with the people we are familiar with, but who are often just as lost and misguided as we are. *No Bueno.* Stop asking people who have never been where you're going for directions. This can further push you back on the time table of self-discovery simply because we allow people to tell us to go Southeast when we should have been heading Northwest.

Also, people tend to limit you based upon the limitations they place upon themselves. Some do it intentionally to stop you from going into higher heights that they themselves are afraid to go, and some do it because they think they are protecting you by warning you not to try, thinking failure is your portion because it was theirs. Either way, God wants you to move forward and not be held hostage to the "what if's."

Ok, I know what you're thinking. You're saying, Now what? How do I go about discovering this hidden treasure in me? Well, remember when I said earlier your treasure map is the Word of God? The next step should be going back to that. Remember, there is no other truth outside of God's Word. Everything we need in life is found in this good book. Hidden treasure is in the inside of you and God wants to reveal it to you so that we can live out our Purpose in life.

God wants to commune with us and tell us the great and hidden things that **Jeremiah 33** talks about. Talk to Him and ask Him what's your Purpose and all the other challenging questions that plague you. After all, treasure hunts can be fun, and God always leaves clues that will help take you to the next level. He's a Good, Good Father…

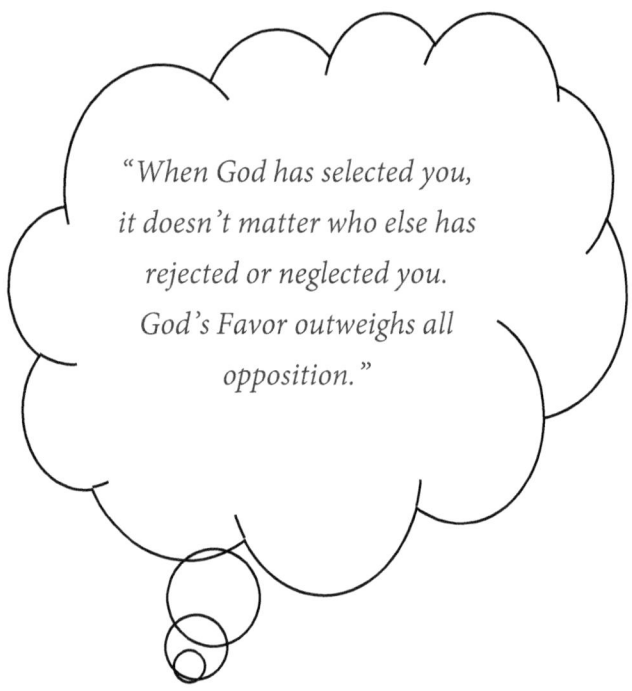

"When God has selected you, it doesn't matter who else has rejected or neglected you. God's Favor outweighs all opposition."

Chapter Seven
"Come Out Come Out Wherever You Are"

Romans 8:19— *"For all creation is waiting eagerly for that future day when God will reveal who his children really are."*

Do you remember the story about Jesus at the wedding in Cana? It's one of the most memorable coming-out parties in history. *John 2:1-11*— *"'The next day there was a wedding celebration in the village of Cana in Galilee. Jesus' mother was there, and Jesus and his disciples were also invited to the celebration.'*

The wine supply ran out during the festivities, so Jesus' mother told him, "They have no more wine."

"Dear woman, that's not our problem," Jesus replied. "My time has not yet come." But his mother told the servants, "Do whatever he tells you."

Standing nearby were six stone water jars, used for Jewish ceremonial washing. Each could hold twenty to thirty gallons. Jesus told the servants, "Fill the jars with water." When the jars had been filled, he said, "Now dip some out, and take it to the master of ceremonies." So, the servants followed his instructions.

When the master of ceremonies tasted the water that was now wine, not knowing where it had come from (though, of course, the servants knew), he called the bridegroom over. "A host always serves the best wine first," he said. "Then, when everyone has had a lot to drink, he brings out the less expensive wine. But you have kept the best until now!"

This miraculous sign at Cana in Galilee was the first time Jesus revealed his glory. And his disciples believed in him."

I just love Mary's confidence in Jesus' ability in that moment. She quickly told the servants, *"Do whatever he tells you."* If you're anything like me, coming out of hiding is the scariest thing ever. I can just imagine the look on Jesus' face when Mary gave the command to the servants. His response is classic — *"Dear woman, that's not our problem. My time has not yet come."* I'm completely sure that I've responded to a person or two in this fashion.

But what happens when it is your time and your hour has come? What happens when, like Joseph, after being enslaved and imprisoned for so many years, your time has finally come to manifest everything God has poured into you during that dark season? What do you do when God no longer wants you *invisible* before men?

We can always say it's not our time, but when God says we must move then get ready because it's time to move. You suddenly go from being an attendant at the wedding to performing a miracle right before the eyes of men. It's time to come out of hiding; it's not only your time, it's now your turn!

In **Romans 8:19**, Paul is talking about all of creation waiting eagerly for that future day when God will reveal who his children really are. Well, for some of you reading this, your time has finally come. Are you prepared to run the race that God has set before you? Are you brave enough to set aside fear and anxiety and step up to the plate when called on?

My grief, my life struggles, my pain, my feelings of rejection didn't disqualify me from being used by God; He was actually equipping and qualifying me, and the same goes for you. I couldn't see it then (definitely not), but God was showing me that I can Trust Him. The dark times when I was faced with death and every other adversity were just my training days for what God was calling me into.

In 2016, my family and I hit rock bottom. I was faced with the most devasting events as a wife and mother, and I wasn't sure my family and I would pull through. We lost everything that we owned (and I mean everything!) We were robbed, became homeless, laid-off from my job and even a few close friends walked away; all in the same month! Once the dust settled and my spiritual eyes regained focus, I was able to see the thief in operation; the events that transpired suddenly, one by one, revealed that the devil was up to something, but God was up to something BIGGER.

Thankfully, at this time in my Christian walk, I knew God loved me and that He would turn things around for my good. I must admit, however, sleeping in my car some nights and other nights in noisy hotels instead of the comfort of my home had me down in the dumps. Especially when I thought about all my clothes, shoes and MY WEDDING RING all gone due to the wickedness in man's heart orchestrated by the devil. Even though I was sure God was up to something, it didn't stop me from crying out to Him in great sorrow; my family was suffering and my son was uncomfortable.

Did I cry some days? Absolutely! Did I wonder why me sometimes? But of course! Did I feel alone? Unfortunately, yes. But I would always remind myself that God can and He will restore. This disaster was an assurance that Greater was on the inside and God was working on pulling it out of me. No more hiding in the shadows; God needed me to arise and manifest. Trouble has a good way of purging and purifying us *only* if we allow God to have His way.

Can I tell you something? Your negative situations will always seem impossible until you come through on the other side. The pressure seemed unbearable, but I was determined to let God complete the good work that He started within me. I wanted nothing that I was going through to be wasted; I just wanted God to get the Glory.

When we recognize that it's not about us, but the greater mission and the souls attached to the mission, we will understand our pain a little bit better. The decision to come out of hiding for the Glory of God won't always be easy but will most definitely be worth it. The *"shadow life"* (as I like to call it) is easy. I used to feel like isolation was my saving grace. Stay away from me and I'll stay from you. Don't talk to me and I won't talk to you. Don't make eye contact or give me advice. Look down when they look up and look up when they look down (lol). It was just a messy way of thinking, and I'm here to tell you it won't work. You need people just as much as they need you, your story, your strength, your brilliance and your prayers. Don't be afraid to come out of the shadows when God says it's time.

In *1 Kings 19*, the great prophet Elijah plunged deep into depression because of some adversity he was faced with.

1 Kings 19:1-8—

"When Ahab got home, he told Jezebel everything Elijah had done, including the way he had killed all the prophets of Baal. So Jezebel sent this message to Elijah: 'May the gods strike me and even kill me if by this time tomorrow I have not killed you just as you killed them.'

Elijah was afraid and fled for his life. He went to Beersheba, a town in Judah, and he left his servant there. Then he went on alone into the wilderness, traveling all day. He sat down under a solitary broom tree and prayed that he might die. "I have had enough, Lord," he said. "Take my life, for I am no better than my ancestors who have already died."

Then he lay down and slept under the broom tree. But as he was sleeping, an angel touched him and told him,

"Get up and eat!" He looked around and there beside his head was some bread baked on hot stones and a jar of water! So he ate and drank and lay down again.

Then the angel of the Lord came again and touched him and said, "Get up and eat some more, or the journey ahead will be too much for you."

So he got up and ate and drank, and the food gave him enough strength to travel forty days and forty nights to Mount Sinai,[a] the mountain of God."

Elijah fell into a place of weariness and thought by hiding in the shadows and asking God to just let him die was the answer. Totally wrong! God allowed him to vent, eat and gain strength for the journey ahead of him. He had more work to be done even though it felt like life was over.

Raise your hand if you can identify with Elijah… I have both hands up.

The great apostle Paul begged three times for God to remove a thorn (stumbling block) from his flesh, but God told Paul in **2 Corinthians 12:9,** *"My grace is all you need. My power works best in weakness."*

After realizing that God wasn't going to remove the thorn, Paul said, *"So now I am glad to boast about my*

weaknesses, so that the power of Christ can work through me."

My motto today is I don't mind being *invisible* as long as it serves Purpose and God gets the Glory. Whether I'm weak or strong, broken or whole, bruised or scorned, when God says it's time to work then it's time to work. And when we forget about the thorn and trust God on our mission, we can then say like Paul, *"I'm glad to boast about my weaknesses, so that the power of Christ can work through me."*

Our failures, weaknesses, mess-ups were all designed to help others, so being perfect is not a requirement and never will be.

1 Corinthians 1:27-28 state that *"Instead, God chose things the world considers foolish in order to shame those who think they are wise. And he chose things that are powerless to shame those who are powerful. God chose things despised by the world,[a] things counted as nothing at all, and used them to bring to nothing what the world considers important."* So, if you have been rejected or despised, welcome to the Winning Team.

Along your journey God will send the right people at the right time to help you see your mission through. Some people will help groom you in your gifting and

point you in the right direction. And God will allow others to see you who would not have even noticed you unless He made the connection.

There's a special lady in my home church who has been a teacher, friend and mother all in one since I first got to my church nine years ago. I call her *special* because you have to be skilled and full of patience to deal with the person I was nine years ago.

At first, it was hard to receive the love she tried over and over to pour over me just because of the broken state I was in. I made up in my mind that I didn't need a mom and dad before and I didn't need one now. I rejected many decent people in that way because I had already grown accustomed to being alone and *invisible*. Over and over she would come to me with an uplifting speech that she refused to watch me sit back and die and that she wouldn't leave me behind. Her constant words of reassurance, her prayers and gifts began to melt my heart and restore hope that God brought me this far for a reason.

Sometimes we think we're completely *invisible* to everyone, but God knows how to make you visible to the ones who need to see you. I'm glad I was able to let my guard down enough so that she could help me.

Mother Grey, as I affectionately love to call her, has been so influential in me wanting to be an aide to even the very people who have caused harm to me and made me feel *invisible.*

According to **Luke 6:22-23**, *"What blessings await you when people hate you and exclude you and mock you and curse you as evil because you follow the Son of Man. When that happens, be happy! Yes, leap for joy! For a great reward awaits you in heaven. And remember, their ancestors treated the ancient prophets that same way."*

Going further down into verses 27 and 28, it says, *"But to you who are willing to listen, I say, love your enemies! Do good to those who hate you. Bless those who curse you. Pray for those who hurt you."*

Ministry is more than just serving the people you like or strangers on the streets, but it's also blessing those who curse you.

Luke 6:33 says, *"If you do good only to those who do good to you, why should you get credit? Even sinners do that much!"*

Mother Grey has taught me how to stand tall, look the enemy directly in his eyes and declare God's Word with Boldness. And through it all, I have had the hard

task of ministering to people who tried to destroy me, undermine me, belittled me and even tried to kill me. She often reminded me that there were people who needed me and that I couldn't give up because there were people waiting for me to manifest. Boy was she right. Her favorite line (which I grew to appreciate) to whom much is given, much is required. I'll let you think about that for a second.

That's why it's best to make moves when God says it's time. Don't jump ahead of the game trying to do things fast to prove people wrong or make yourself seem more valuable than others. There's no better coming-out party than the one God throws for us. On your coming-out day, you don't have to make any public announcements for yourself, but God Himself will do the announcing just like He did with Jesus the day he was baptized in the Jordan River.

Matthew 3:13-17—

"Then Jesus went from Galilee to the Jordan River to be baptized by John. But John tried to talk him out of it. 'I am the one who needs to be baptized by you,' he said, 'so why are you coming to me?'

COME OUT COME OUT WHEREVER YOU ARE

But Jesus said, "It should be done, for we must carry out all that God requires.[a]" So John agreed to baptize him.

After his baptism, as Jesus came up out of the water, the heavens were opened[b] and he saw the Spirit of God descending like a dove and settling on him. And a voice from heaven said, 'This is my dearly loved Son, who brings me great joy.'"

Always remember, just because God announces you doesn't mean people will start to acknowledge you or give you pats on the back. You must understand that rejection is a part of the process from start to finish. Jesus was rejected even to the cross; His own friends (disciples) abandoned Him. People He healed and cast out devils from turned their backs on Him. But, Jesus is our prime example of how to walk according to the call and not according to likes on social media. You must ask yourself some tough questions. Why am I doing what I'm doing? And if you find yourself always wanting people's approval, then there are deeper issues at hand that you MUST take to the Lord in prayer.

Jesus came out of hiding, but He still was *invisible* (unseen for who He truly was and His purpose.) So, remember, coming out or being released by God to work in the Kingdom doesn't mean lights, camera, action or sudden acceptance from everyone. Always remember whose you are, who you are and your reason for being who you are. Keeping this as a focal point will always keep you on track.

"I give because I know how it feels to want."

Letter from Keshia

To My Dear Sweet Reader:

I just wanted to remind you that although your journey to healing and moving forward in God may start here, it will most certainly not end here. There will be times you run and run well. There will also be times when you'll walk or speed walk. And there will be times where you might fall and may not have the strength to get back up again. These various stages are normal, and you can and will overcome. Get around some good accountability partners, stay in the Word of God and in prayer and watch God move you into a place of wellness that you've never imagined. Remember you are important. You are valuable, and I am praying for you. Now go Forth and Prosper 😊

Love,

K. Staple

Scriptures to Remember

Isaiah 41:13

"For I hold you by your right hand--I, the LORD your God. And I say to you, 'Don't be afraid. I am here to help you.'"

Lamentations 3:22-23

"The LORD'S loving kindnesses indeed never cease, For His compassions never fail. They are new every morning; Great is Your faithfulness."

Psalm 62:8

"O my people, trust in him at all times. Pour out your heart to him, for God is our refuge."

Psalm 103:13

"The LORD is like a father to his children, tender and compassionate to those who fear him."

SCRIPTURES TO REMEMBER

John 1:12

"But to all who believed him and accepted him, he gave the right to become children of God."

Psalm 63:3

"Your unfailing love is better than life itself; how I praise you!"

Hebrew 13:5

"Don't love money; be satisfied with what you have. For God has said, 'I will never fail you. I will never abandon you.'"

2 Peter 3:9

"The Lord isn't really being slow about his promise, as some people think. No, he is being patient for your sake. He does not want anyone to be destroyed, but wants everyone to repent."

1 John 3:16

"We know what real love is because Jesus gave up his life for us. So we also ought to give up our lives for our brothers and sisters."

SCRIPTURES TO REMEMBER

Matthew 11:29

"Take my yoke upon you. Let me teach you, because I am humble and gentle at heart, and you will find rest for your souls."

Isaiah 54:10

"For the mountains may move and the hills disappear, but even then, my faithful love for you will remain. My covenant of blessing will never be broken, says the LORD, who has mercy on you."

Ephesians 4:1

"Therefore I, a prisoner for serving the Lord, beg you to lead a life worthy of your calling, for you have been called by God."

1 John 3:1

"See how very much our Father loves us, for he calls us his children, and that is what we are! But the people who belong to this world don't recognize that we are God's children because they don't know him."

SCRIPTURES TO REMEMBER

Psalm 103:2-5

"Let all that I am praise the LORD; may I never forget the good things he does for me. He forgives all my sins and heals all my diseases. He redeems me from death and crowns me with love and tender mercies. He fills my life with good things. My youth is renewed like the eagle's!"

Isaiah 53:6

"All of us, like sheep, have strayed away. We have left God's paths to follow our own. Yet the LORD laid on him the sins of us all."

Matthew 28:20

"Teach these new disciples to obey all the commands I have given you. And be sure of this: 'I am with you always, even to the end of the age.'"

Jeremiah 33:3

"Ask me and I will tell you remarkable secrets you do not know about things to come."

John 15:9

"I have loved you even as the Father has loved me. Remain in my love."

Luke 6:27-28

"But to you who are willing to listen, I say, love your enemies! Do good to those who hate you. Bless those who curse you. Pray for those who hurt you."

Matthew 21:42

"Then Jesus asked them, 'Didn't you ever read this in the Scriptures? The stone that the builders rejected has now become the cornerstone. This is the LORD's doing, and it is wonderful to see.'"

1 John 1:9

"But if we confess our sins to him, he is faithful and just to forgive us our sins and to cleanse us from all wickedness."

About the Author

Keshia Staple was born and raised in Miami, Florida and is a proud wife, mother, mentor and ministry leader. Keshia is President of Stapled 2gether Ministries, an organization that promotes being true in your walk with God and allowing Him to mend the broken pieces of our lives that may occur through disappointments, loneliness, betrayal, misguidance, fear and anxiety. Keshia loves to inspire and bring hope to the poor in spirit using the powerful message of Jesus Christ.

www.ingramcontent.com/pod-product-compliance
Lightning Source LLC
LaVergne TN
LVHW051152080426
835508LV00021B/2591